D0646382

Provinces and Territories of Canada

NUNAVUT

— *"Explore Canada's Arctic"* —

Published by Weigl Educational Publishers Limited
6325 10 Street SE
Calgary, Alberta
T2H 2Z9

www.weigl.com

Library and Archives Canada Cataloguing in Publication data available upon request.
Fax 403-233-7769 for the attention of the Publishing Records department.

ISBN 978-1-55388-979-3 (hard cover)
ISBN 978-1-55388-992-2 (soft cover)

Printed in the United States of America
1 2 3 4 5 6 7 8 9 0 13 12 11 10 09

Editor: Heather C. Hudak
Design: Terry Paulhus

All of the Internet URLs given in the book were valid at the time of publication. However, due to the dynamic nature
of the Internet, some addresses may have changed, or sites may have ceased to exist since publication. While the author
and publisher regret any inconvenience this may cause readers, no responsibility for any such changes can be accepted
by either the author or the publisher.

Every reasonable effort has been made to trace ownership and to obtain permission to reprint copyright material. The publishers
would be pleased to have any errors or omissions brought to their attention so that they may be corrected in subsequent printings.

Weigl acknowledges Getty Images as its primary image supplier for this title.
Hudson's Bay Company Archives, Provincial Archives of Manitoba: page 30 top.

We gratefully acknowledge the financial support of the Government of Canada through the Book Publishing Industry Development Program
(BPIDP) for our publishing activities.

Contents

Nunavut

Before April 1999, Nunavut was a part of the Northwest Territories. Since then, this huge land mass has separated from the Northwest Territories to become a territory of its own. It is by far the largest of any province or territory in Canada, making up about one-fifth of the country's area. Nunavut straddles four time zones as it spreads over the Arctic mainland and islands. Baffin and Ellesmere Islands are now a part of Nunavut, as are the Keewatin, Baffin, and Kitikmeot areas of the Northwest Territories. To the West, the Inuvik and Fort Smith regions establish borders with Nunavut. Manitoba, Hudson Bay, and Quebec border it to the south, and Baffin Bay and the Labrador Sea border it to the east. Glaciers up to 5 kilometres thick moved across Nunavut during the last Ice Age. As they moved, they scraped the rock bare and then retreated. In some places, they left behind ridges of gravel, called **eskers**. Icecaps 2 kilometres thick still cover much of Ellesmere Island and parts of Devon and Baffin islands.

Nunavut stretches across a great deal of the Canadian North. It covers almost 2 million square kilometres and is 2,400 kilometres at its widest.

Baffin Island is the largest island in Canada and the fifth largest island in the world. It is home to Nunavut's capital and many other communities. The island's landscape is made up of tundra, rivers, and glaciers.

Getting to Nunavut, and getting around in Nunavut, can be challenging. Due to the territory's rugged terrain, its huge area, and the limited number of people who travel in the North, there are no railways in Nunavut. Outside the towns, there are only about 21 kilometres of road on Baffin Island.

Boat travel is another method of transportation, but it is limited by the ice that covers much of the water. However, freezing weather can be helpful to other modes of transportation. People can use snowmobiles to get around when the land is snow-covered and the waterways are frozen.

Icecaps and glaciers cover about 150,000 square kilometres of Nunavut.

Iqaluit is the capital of Nunavut.

Nunavut's vast land region and extensive wilderness is inhabited mostly by Inuit. The struggle to establish an Inuit territory began between the Inuit and the federal government in 1976. It took until 1992 before both sides could agree on all issues, including the western border. In 1993, the land claim agreement was signed, setting the creation of a new territory in motion. Nunavut became an official territory on April 1, 1999.

The land claim that went with this agreement was the largest in Canadian history. It gave the Inuit control over 351,000 square kilometres of Nunavut. It also gave the Inuit mining rights in certain areas, hunting and fishing rights, and payment of about $1.15 billion to the Nunavut Trust over a period of 14 years. The trust is in charge of protecting and building on this money to ensure a strong Nunavut for years to come.

GET THE FACTS

The territory's motto is "Nunavut Saginvut," which means "Nunavut our strength."

Although it covers four time zones, Nunavut uses Central time.

When travelling to Nunavut, visitors from Europe fly to Greenland, where they connect for a flight to Iqaluit.

The introduction of Nunavut marked the first time Canada's map had changed since Newfoundland joined Confederation in 1949.

LAND AND CLIMATE

Nunavut's landscape is a mixture of mountains, **fjords**, lakes, and tundra. The mainland and Baffin Island are part of the **Canadian Shield**. Some of the rocks in this area are more than one billion years old. Farther north, the shield is covered with layers of younger rock. Much of the territory's land was shaped by glaciers. The ice sheets reached the Arctic Ocean coastline, creating deep valleys and fjords.

On Axel Heiberg Island, Baffin Island, and the eastern part of Ellesmere Island, mountains range from 1,500 to 2,000 metres in height. The rest of Nunavut is a high, flat plateau gashed by ravines and covered in lakes, **muskeg**, and swamps. The islands to the west are low.

Nunavut's ground is permanently frozen, sometimes to a depth of 500 metres. A thin layer of the surface, called the active layer, thaws in summer but re-freezes in winter.

Most of Nunavut's many rivers are on the mainland. The Back and the Coppermine Rivers flow northward into the Arctic Ocean. The Thelon, Kazan and Dubawnt Rivers all eventually flow into Hudson Bay. Since the land is low-lying and irregular, the rivers often widen out to form lakes. The biggest lake on the mainland is Dubawnt Lake.

Most of the rivers on Baffin Island are on the west side. These rivers are short because the sea is never very far away. Nunavut's two largest lakes, Nettilling and Amadjuak, are on Baffin Island. Ellesmere Island also boasts large lakes. Lake Hazen is 72 kilometres long and nearly 10 kilometres wide. It is the largest lake in the area.

In winter, the lakes and the ground are so frozen that they can be used as temporary roads.

Nunavut's ground is frozen for most of the year, which is an indication of how cold the territory can get. Winters in Nunavut are very long and cold. Daily January temperatures average −20° Celsius on south Baffin Island and about −37° C on north Ellesmere Island. Nunavut's short summers can average 21° C, and for a short time, flowers can bloom. However, cold prevails, and it is possible to build igloos by November.

Nunavut's highest mountain is Mount Barbeau, on northern Ellesmere Island. It stands 2,616 m high.

Wilberforce Falls, on the Hood River near Bathurst Inlet, is the highest waterfall north of the Arctic Circle.

Annual precipitation in Nunavut ranges from 600 millimetres in the south to less than 100 millimetres in the north. Some areas in Nunavut get less precipitation than the Sahara Desert.

Many of Nunavut's lakes do not even have names.

The coldest temperature ever recorded in Nunavut was −57.8° C at Shepherd Bay in 1973. The warmest temperature was 33.9° C in Arviat, also in 1973.

NATURAL RESOURCES

Much of Nunavut is remote, making it difficult to transport natural resources to other parts of the country and world.

The Canadian Shield contains many minerals, but finding and exploiting them in such a remote place as Nunavut is difficult. The expense of transportation and the freezing weather are big challenges to the mining industry. The lead and zinc mines of Nanisivik and Polaris are almost always icebound. Only in summer can ships bring in supplies and carry the ore out.

KEEP CONNECTED
For more about mining in Nunavut, visit **www.miningnorth.com**.

From January to April, the only way for the Lupin gold mine on Contwoyto Lake to send its products out is on special winter roads.

Nunavut's harsh climate and rugged terrain is a challenge for companies that want to mine for natural resources.

Mining activities began in the barren lands along the Thelon River after diamonds were discovered there. Nunavut's first diamond mine, Jericho, opened in 2006. Though it closed in 2008, the potential for mining diamonds remains. Nunavut also has large oil and gas deposits in the northern Arctic Ocean. These reserves can only be developed when world oil prices make it possible. Otherwise, the expense of drilling in this area is much too great.

GET THE FACTS

To make life more enjoyable for the miners, facilities at Polaris Mine include a coffee shop, a swimming pool, and a golf club.

There are no forests or farms in Nunavut.

The most important fish in northern waters is the arctic char.

The Lupin and Polaris mines are called fly-in, fly-out operations. There is no community nearby for workers to live in.

PLANTS AND ANIMALS

Despite the cold climate, the tundra comes alive with flowers in the summer.

The purple saxifrage is the official flower of Nunavut.

Nunavut's infertile, shallow soil is frozen all winter, making life hard for plants. The few plants that live in the territory survive the bitter winters and summers by crowding together. They find shelter in rock crevices or by lying flat to the ground. Lichens and mosses, with some spindly bushes, cover the tundra.

About 200 species of flowers, including dandelions and buttercups, survive to bloom in the long hours of summer sunlight. People and animals take advantage of the blossoming plants. The Inuit eat blueberries, cranberries, and crowberries, while the caribou feast on reindeer lichen.

Polar bears in the Nunavut area spend most of the year roaming the sea ice.

Nunavut is home to about half the world's polar bears. They feed on the ringed seals that live in the area. Caribou are also abundant, with more than 750,000 living in the territory. The Arctic waters are home to beluga whales, **narwhals**, and **bowheads**. Seals and walruses are common Nunavut residents. Hares, squirrels, foxes, weasels, and wolves also make their homes in the area.

Only a few birds survive on the cold tundra. Snowy owls, eider ducks, and gyrfalcons brave the elements and are permanent residents of the territory. Many seabirds will also come north in the spring and summer to breed on the rocky coasts. There is a delicate balance in these barren lands, and each plant and animal plays an important role in the food chain to keep the **ecosystem** strong.

KEEP CONNECTED

Information about Nunavut's wildlife conservation programs can be found at www.nwmb.com/english.

The rough-legged hawk is one type of bird found in Nunavut. It nests on cliff sides and hunts in the open tundra.

The rock ptarmigan is Nunavut's official bird.

Muskoxen are found both on the mainland and on most Arctic islands. At one point, the muskox was endangered, but now there are about 47,000 roaming the Nunavut area.

The students and teachers at Joamie School in Iqaluit are dedicated to the preservation of Nunavut's environment. The school has been named Canada's first Earth School.

The Thelon Wildlife Sanctuary is one of the largest and most remote wildlife refuges in North America.

There are different kinds of caribou in Nunavut. The woodland caribou migrate south to the forests, barren-ground caribou stay on the tundra, and Peary caribou live on the northern islands.

Nunavut is located almost entirely above the tree line.

TOURISM

National parks, such as Auyuittuq, are popular destinations for tourists.

Many people travel to Nunavut to take in its unique scenery. In fact, tourism brings about $30 million into the economy every year. Wilderness canoe trips down the Thelon River allow visitors close-up views of muskox, caribou, white arctic wolves, golden eagles, rough-legged hawks, and owls. Tourists can marvel at the spectacular wilderness, mountain fortresses, and fascinating wildlife of Auyuittuq National Park Reserve and Ellesmere Island National Park Reserve.

In summer, visitors can venture to the floe edge, where the ice meets the open sea. Here, they can see the shrimp that come to eat plankton, and the seals and whales that feed on the shrimp. There may even be polar bears lurking close by.

Visitor centres in various communities have demonstrations of everyday activities that took place in traditional Inuit summer camps. Others interpret the traditions of 1,000 years of Inuit life in Nunavut. The Nunatta Sunakkutaangit Museum in Iqaluit has displays that explain the history of south Baffin Island. It also exhibits a variety of Inuit art and clothing.

The spring ice floes are not only a tourist attraction. Polar bears, seals and walruses use them as a hunting base or to relax in the sun.

Fox are trapped for their furs. The remains of stone fox traps and thousand- year-old dwellings line the coast, attracting history buffs.

Inuit artists use traditional methods to make crafts. Nunavut has tourist camps where visitors can learn this type of craft-making.

KEEP CONNECTED

Inuit art ranges from paintings and carvings to jewellery and dolls. In many cases, the art is a reflection of Inuit ways of life. All Inuit artwork has an igloo symbol on it to show its authenticity. Find out more about Inuit art at **www.uqqurmiut.com**.

Once the new government of Nunavut took power, office buildings and houses were needed to accommodate the people employed. The construction industry continues to grow because of the business that self-government has generated. Houses are also needed because Inuit continue to move to where the jobs are being created.

The sale of Inuit art is an important industry in Nunavut. A large part of the territory's economy is based on exporting this art to other places around the world. Until the 1940s, Inuit art was almost completely unavailable to those outside the Arctic. Through marketing projects, the popularity and demand for Inuit art spread all over the world. Today, a large number of Inuit artists earn their living by selling their work.

Very few industries have developed in Nunavut due to the territory's remote location and the high cost of transportation.

Transportation is provided by bush, charter, and scheduled airlines.

Despite the cost of imported items, stores still carry candy, books, and even movies.

Almost no goods are produced for sale in Nunavut. Many items have to be imported from the south, which makes them very expensive. For example, imported foods cost about one-third more than they do in southern Canada due to the added shipping costs. In more remote communities, such as Grise Fiord, costs are even higher. For this reason, locally caught fish and **game** are very important. Food that is caught locally and eaten traditionally is called country food. It makes up more than half of what is eaten in Nunavut.

The governments of Canada and Nunavut are the biggest employers in the territory. The treaty that made Nunavut a territory states that 85 percent of government workers are to be Inuit. The treaty also says that Inuit companies must have increased participation in government contracts. The government hires private companies to build office complexes. Other companies provide services, including retail stores and taxis, to accommodate the needs of government employees and other residents.

KEEP CONNECTED

The service industry is important in Nunavut. People working in the service sector do things for other people. Waiters, doctors, government officials, sales clerks, and lawyers are all service employees. For more about services in Nunavut, visit http://cgs.gov.nu.ca/en/services-communities.

Health care services in Nunavut are provided by the government. There is one hospital in Iqaluit and about 14 community health centres throughout Nunavut's regions. These centres offer nursing, children's welfare, and counselling services.

Five percent of government employees work in education, which is also managed directly in the regions. All communities have schools, and the main community college in Nunavut is the Arctic College in Iqaluit. The institute provides guidance in traditional knowledge, science, research, and technology. To maintain Inuit traditions and ways of life, the government is building an Inuktituk curriculum and training Inuit teachers. Providing classes in Inuktituk are necessary because it is the working language of the government.

Wages in Nunavut are higher than in other places in Canada to make up for the territory's high cost of living.

GET THE FACTS

The Igloolik Research Institute is part of the Nunavik Arctic College.

In the ice-free season, boat transportation is very important because it can carry larger cargoes.

Iqaluit's Parnaivik Building is a mini-mall that houses government offices, a coffee shop, and a fabric store.

Nunavut gets its news from CBC North and three newspapers.

FIRST NATIONS

The Thule may have been the first peoples to use dogsleds. Dogsleds are still used by the Inuit today.

The pre-Dorset people arrived in the Canadian Arctic about 4,500 years ago. They were named for the island of Cape Dorset, where artifacts from their people were found. These people formed small groups to follow the caribou and seal, and they used tools and weapons made of flint and bone. They lived in tents made of animal skin.

The Dorset people emerged about 2,500 years ago. In the spring, they hunted walruses, caribou, small mammals, and seals. They caught fish in the summer and trapped seals in the fall and winter. Some of the food they caught was stored in **caches** for the long winter seasons.

The word "Nunavut" is Inuktitut for "our land." Iqaluit means "place of fish."

Nunavut's present-day Inuit are descended from the Thule, who originally migrated from Alaska. The summer homes of the Thule were tents made of animal skins, but their winter homes were solid structures. The Thule's winter homes were sunk into the ground. They had a stone floor, a whale bone or stone frame, and a roof of sealskin. Houses were covered with sod and heated by seal or whale oil burned in a stone lamp. The Thule's graves consisted of piles of stones, with the remains of the person and their belongings placed nearby.

Inuktitut is the official language of the Inuit.

The Thule hunted game with bows and arrows or spears. In summer, they hunted whales from kayaks and fished with **tridents** and hooks.

EXPLORERS

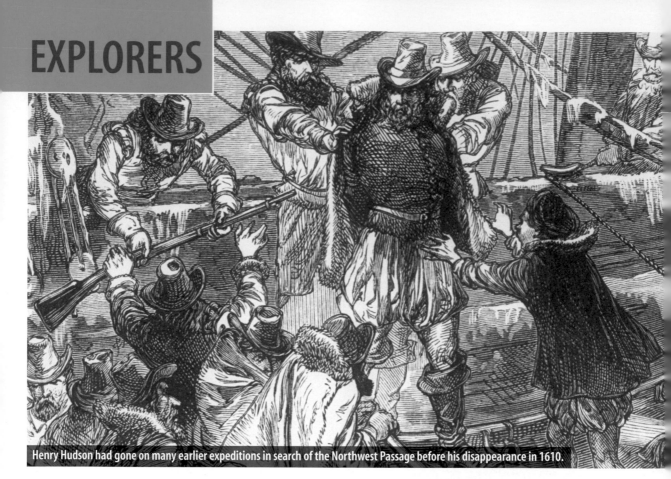

Henry Hudson had gone on many earlier expeditions in search of the Northwest Passage before his disappearance in 1610.

The first European to reach Nunavut was an English explorer named Sir Martin Frobisher. He sailed west from the Atlantic Ocean in search of the **Northwest Passage**. In 1576, he landed on Baffin Island and named the area Frobisher Strait. He returned to the area two more times in search of gold.

The search for the Northwest Passage brought many other explorers to the area. In the 1580s, John Davis tried his luck at finding the passage, but ice floes blocked his route. In 1610, Henry Hudson believed he had succeeded in finding the Northwest Passage when he entered the bay now named for him. His ship became iced in, and the cold climate led to an angry crew. His crew **mutinied**, and Hudson and several others were set adrift in a small boat. They were never seen again.

Frobisher took what he thought was gold back to England. It proved to be iron pyrite or "fool's gold."

John Franklin has been credited with laying the groundwork for the discovery of the Northwest Passage. Franklin made two trips to northern Canada. These trips helped pave the way for the exploration of Canada's northern lands. He explored and mapped much of the Far North. These efforts eventually assisted in the discovery of the Northwest Passage.

In 1845, Franklin set out with 129 British navy sailors. His ships became stuck in ice, and the crews were lost when they left the ships. The British Navy mapped most of the Arctic islands and straits while searching for Franklin and his crew. They were later found to have died in the freezing and difficult conditions.

Between the years of 1903 and 1906, Roald Amundsen became the first person to successfully navigate a ship though the Northwest Passage.

Roald Amundsen is well known around the world, but he is especially important to Canadian history. On a voyage lasting from 1903 to 1906, he became the first person to navigate the Northwest Passage. Amundsen was the first to finally conquer the freezing temperatures and massive icebergs of the Arctic water and sail over the northernmost of North America. In doing so, he realized the dreams of centuries of explorers and captured the imaginations of people around the world.

GET THE FACTS

The strait between Greenland and Baffin Island is named for John Davis.

The crews of Davis' four ships played a soccer game on the ice with the Inuit.

At Arctic Bay, which is north of the Arctic Circle, the sun rises on May 4 and does not set again until August 8. In the winter, the sun sets on November 11, and it is not seen again until January 30.

European whaling crews were eager to recruit the Inuit because of their excellent hunting skills.

The central Arctic is so vast that there were probably many Inuit who, by 1900, had never seen a European.

Basque and Portuguese people came to Nunavut in the 1500s for fish and whales, but they did not settle there. Whalers continued to come for four centuries in search of whale oil and baleen. Whale oil was used in European and North American lamps, and baleen, the bony plates from the whale, did many of the jobs that plastic does today.

By the 1850s, whalers had established whaling stations and spent the winter in the Arctic so they could be there when the season began. This changed some traditional Inuit ways. Many Inuit began to stay and work with the whalers instead of going inland in the summer to hunt. The Inuit did most of the whaling and traded oil for European goods. Guns, metal pots, cloth, utensils, and alcohol became important to many Inuit communities. Contact with Europeans had a price, however. Many Inuit died from diseases brought by Europeans.

Reverend Edmund Peck helped develop a written form of Inuktituk. He also set up the first permanent mission in the area.

Missionaries followed the whalers and traders to the eastern Arctic. It was their aim to convert the Inuit from their belief in **shamans** to Christianity. According to traditional Inuit belief, shamans are men or women who bring health and prosperity and know the secrets of magic and religion.

Reverend Edmund Peck set up the first mission in 1894 on Black Lead Island near Pangnirtung in the Cumberland Sound. He helped develop a written form of Inuktitut using symbols. He then translated the Bible into this Inuit language. The Inuit called Reverend Peck "Uqammak," which means "the one who speaks well." The script he developed is still used today.

KEEP CONNECTED

The Inuit played important roles as guides, hunters, and interpreters for the Europeans. Information about Inuit history can be found at **www.civilization.ca/cmc/home/cmc-home**. Type "Inuit history" into the search engine, and click on the first link.

Other missionaries travelled to Inuit camps spreading the word of Christianity and discouraging the use of shamans. The Inuit adopted many aspects of Christianity, and sometimes they formed their own religions by mixing various religious ideas. At the same time, they lost many of their traditional beliefs. Inuit names were too hard for missionaries to pronounce, so they gave the Inuit biblical names. The government simply gave them numbers stamped on a disc and looped around their necks.

Churches set up the first schools and hospitals. During the 1920s and 1930s, five **residential** schools were established. Children as young as five were taken away from their own communities to learn the Christian way of life. Education by the missionaries continued until the 1960s when the government began to build schools.

The Canadian government set up North-West Mounted Police posts when American whalers and explorers from other countries entered the Arctic. The government wanted to protect Canada's claim on the land. Today, the RCMP have posts across Nunavut to protect the region.

The majority of Canada's Inuit live in Nunavut.

Before 1999, the Northwest Territories had two main regions. The west was the partly forested Mackenzie Valley, populated by Dene, Métis, Inuit, and non-Aboriginal people. The east was mainly barren, and 85 percent of its inhabitants were Inuit.

In 1999, the east became Nunavut, and was divided into three regions. Eastern and northern Nunavut are called Qikiqtaaluk, or the Baffin region. Southern Nunavut and the area near Hudson Bay are called Kivalliq, or Keewatin. Central and western Nunavut are called Kitikmeot.

The Baffin region, which includes almost all the islands, is the largest and the most heavily populated region. There are twenty-five communities in Nunavut. Eight of them are on Baffin Island.

Iqaluit has about 6,184 residents.

GET THE FACTS

The Inuit make up 85 percent of Nunavut's population. The rest of the population is made up mostly of people of British and European descent.

There are about 29,474 people living in Nunavut.

Until 1987, Iqaluit was known as Frobisher Bay.

Canada's most northerly community is Grise Fiord, on Ellesmere Island.

English is spoken by 24 percent of Nunavut's population, and French is spoken by about 2 percent.

People in Nunavut have been able to balance tradition with European culture. For example, children's school years are based around the hunting seasons.

Inuit peoples live across the northern Arctic, from Alaska to Greenland, in eight main groups. They speak up to 20 different dialects of Inuktituk and can usually understand each other. About 71 percent of Nunavut's population speak Inuktitut.

POLITICS AND GOVERNMENT

A territory is different from a province. A province owns its own land and has powers that are set out in Confederation. A territory, on the other hand, is created through federal law, and the federal government owns the land. The federal government can make decisions in a territory on matters such as education, whereas provinces can make their own decisions and policies. A territory cannot vote on changes to the Canadian Constitution.

The Inuit worked with the Government of Canada from 1976 to 1992 to reach an agreement about the new territory. In 1982, the people of the Northwest Territories were asked to vote on whether their territory should be split into two parts. The residents agreed that the Northwest Territories should become two territories. In 1993, after years of negotiation, a land claim agreement was signed. The agreement gave the Inuit control over 351,000 square kilometres of Nunavut. The Inuit people were also granted the fishing, hunting, and mining rights for the territory. On April 1, 1999, Nunavut became an official territory.

The government of Nunavut is based in Iqaluit.

The government building in Iqaluit has wooden arches formed to represent an igloo. It also has sealskin-covered benches instead of desks in the meeting chamber.

The Nunavut territorial government has an elected Legislative Assembly, with 19 members and a cabinet of ministers overseeing the activities of ten departments. Some departments, like the Department of Culture, Language, Elders, and Youth, are concerned with maintaining Inuit traditions. The departments and agencies are spread around the communities of Nunavut so that they will all receive a share of the money granted to the territory by the federal government. This will also allow regions to make decisions according to their local needs.

GET THE FACTS

After Nunavut became its own territory, there was some debate over who—Nunavut or the Northwest Territories—would get to keep the polar bear-shaped license plate. It was finally agreed that the territories would share the shape.

Paul Ikalik became the first premier of Nunavut in 1999.

The gold and blue in Nunavut's flag symbolize the riches of land, sea, and sky. The red in the flag is an indication of the territory's ties with Canada.

Elders, with their skills and traditional knowledge, play an important role in all areas of Inuit life and politics.

CULTURAL GROUPS

The Inuit way of life stems from an ancient society in which survival depended both on teamwork and on respect for one's natural surroundings. Working together was vital to surviving in the harsh climate of the North. Today, the Inuit in Nunavut continue to respect their environment and to believe in the importance of sharing. The sharing of game and fish among families is still a vital part of Inuit society. Many Inuit believe that food tastes better when it is shared with family and friends.

Food in Nunavut is very different from most Canadian dishes. Among the most popular foods are arctic char, caribou, and muskox, which tastes like beef. Raw seal is a traditional dish. During a meal, men and women get different parts of the seal. Other favourites include maktaaq, which consists of the outer skin of the whale served raw, and dips such as *aalu*, which is made up of caribou or seal meat, fat, blood, and ptarmigan intestines. *Misiraq*, which is aged seal blubber, and *nirukkaq*, which are the contents of a caribou's stomach, are other unique dips.

An expert seal hunter lunges his spear at a seal just beneath the water's surface.

Inuktitut is spoken throughout Nunavut, but **dialects** and accents vary from region to region. In Kitikmeot, or western Nunavut, the name of the Inuit language is Inuinnaqtun.

A large portion of the Inuit population in Nunavut speaks English, but all over the territory, Inuit strive to keep their traditional language alive. They have also added new words to their vocabulary, some of which are related to the English word. For example, when European explorers arrived, the Inuit were introduced to items such as sugar and paper. They adopted these words into their own language, and now *sukaq* and *paipaaq* are Inuktitut words.

The Inuit burn whale or seal oil in a stone lamp, or qulliq, to heat and light igloos. As a symbol, it represents the light and warmth of the family and community.

Snowmobiles, rifles, schools, and permanent housing have had a great influence on the Inuit way of life. Although older Inuit speak only Inuktituk, most younger adults are comfortable in both the Inuit and mainstream Canadian worlds. More and more, young people are taking advantage of modern technology, including the Internet.

Many families gather to enjoy raw seal during a communal feast celebrating the Christmas season.

Some Inuit still follow the traditional life, while many others have moved into the world of business, helping to develop Nunavut through politics, teaching, medicine, and broadcasting.

The word Inuit means "people" in Inuktitut. Inuk means "one person."

Nunavut's environment is so fragile in places that visitors are asked not to pick berries without guidance from local residents.

The Inuit show their love for children very openly, allowing

relatives to adopt one of their children if they have many. Traditionally, elders name the babies after relatives or people they admire.

ARTS AND ENTERTAINMENT

Art is a valued part of Inuit life. It ranges from sculpture and fabric-making to art prints and jewellery. The Inuit carve in soapstone, **serpentine**, marble, ivory, and bone. Early sculptures usually represented local activities, mythical figures, or the shapes and spirits of animals. Printmaking, which is a growing Inuit art form, also tells stories of wilderness survival, traditional myths, and shamans.

Another traditional art form among the Inuit is storytelling. Much of Inuit history is preserved through this favourite pastime. At celebrations, people tell stories with important themes and messages or that detail the hardships of hunting. Celebrations also involve singing, drumming, and plenty of food.

Music has always been an important part of Inuit life. For centuries, drum dancing has welcomed visitors and celebrated births, weddings, deaths, and successful hunts. Singers, usually women, would sit in a circle while drummers played. Men would volunteer to dance in the circle. Drum dancing is now performed mainly for tourists and on ceremonial occasions.

Inukshuks are human-like stone figures that are believed to have guided travellers and hunters.

Another fascinating form of Inuit music is throat singing. This incredible art form involves two or three singers, usually women. These women stand face to face and make rhythmic noises by breathing out from the throat. The sound that resonates between the singers often represents the sounds of birds or animals.

Drumming is a traditional Inuit form of music.

Some of Nunavut's musicians have earned acclaim beyond the territory. Arviat's Susan Aglukark has won fame all over Canada by mixing Inuit chants with pop music in English and Inuktituk. Her songs discuss the discrimination against Inuit peoples and her own personal tragedies and successes. They also touch on Inuit rituals and values and the hardships of northern life. Aglukark has won an Aboriginal Achievement Award and a Juno Award for best new solo artist. The throat singing duo, Tudjaat, has appeared in concert and on record with Susan Aglukark.

GET THE FACTS

With the introduction of modern tools, carving became an easier and more profitable industry for Inuit artists.

European whalers and traders brought the country fiddle, accordion, and mouth organ to Nunavut. Country and western and gospel music are also very popular.

Square dancing is a popular pastime all over Nunavut.

Pioneer Inuit musicians, such as Charlie Panigoniak, have a wide following of fans.

Inuit music has been brought to wide audiences through media coverage and events such as The Great Northern Arts Festival and the Inummarit Music Festival.

Women used to make dolls to help teach their children about Inuit ways of life. They also occasionally traded these dolls with whalers in the area. Today, doll-making has been raised to an art form.

Susan Aglukark's music incorporates many aspects of traditional Inuit music such as rhythmic drumming.

Experts can tell where a carving was made. Pangnirtung stone is black, Arviat stone is grey, and Repulse Bay stone is dark green.

Inuit art became known to the rest of the world around 1948, when a young Toronto artist named James A. Houston realized that the Inuit could sell their art to solve some of their economic problems.

SPORTS

Cross-country skiing is a popular pastime among Nunavut's residents and visitors. Skiers can witness Nunavut's wildlife up close as they glide along. Some athletes also enjoy downhill skiing.

Nunavut residents enjoy playing basketball outdoors during the brief summer season.

Activities such as camping, kayaking, dogsledding, snowmobiling, hunting, and fishing are considered recreational sports in southern Canada. In Nunavut, they are more than that. These sports are a part of the traditional Inuit way of life. The people of Nunavut also enjoy sports such as hockey, curling, and badminton. They even enjoy a round of golf now and then.

Traditional Inuit games are both a diversion to Nunavut's long, cold months and a way to stay fit. Many of the games are based on skills that were once needed to survive in the Arctic. One of the most popular games is the high kick. Among the types of high kicks are the two-foot and one-foot high kicks, and the Alaskan high kick. The one and two-foot high kicks involve jumping up, kicking an object that is suspended in the air, and landing in a certain way. The Alaskan high kick requires great skill and wrist strength, as part of the kick involves balancing the entire body on one wrist.

The Inuit play a traditional tossing game.

Toonik Tyme is Nunavut's largest festival of traditional Inuit games. The games take place in Iqaluit every spring. Igloo building, snowmobile and dog-team races, entertainment, and feasting are all a part of the fun.

Other important athletic competitions are held throughout the territory. The Midnight Sun Marathon celebrates the longest day of the year and attracts runners from all over the world. One hundred runners from Canada, the United States, Europe, and Australia are invited to run in the 10-km, 32-km, 42-km, or 84-km races between Arctic Bay and Nanisivik. The Midnight Sun Golf Tournament at Pelly Bay is played on a homemade course. Golfers tee off on rugs loaned by local families.

KEEP CONNECTED

For more information about Inuit games and sports, visit www.virtualmuseum.ca/Exhibitions/Traditions/English/inuit_games.html.

The kayak is a closed-deck hunting canoe, usually designed for one person. A traditional kayak is made of driftwood with willow ribs and covered in de-haired sealskin or caribou skin.

In the summer, the Kitikmeot Northern Games have unique Good Man and Good Woman contests in family skills. These skills include tea boiling, duck plucking, seal skinning, and **bannock** making.

GET THE FACTS

The Inuit made sealskin balls stuffed with hair or moss. The balls were used to play different games.

Every two years, Nunavut's athletes join athletes from other Arctic regions for the Arctic Winter Games.

Nunavut communities have a Hamlet Day to celebrate spring. It is almost always a combination of traditional and modern games and races. Some even have "blindfolded human dog team" races.

Each society brings a small group of cultural artists to the Arctic Winter Games. A display of visual arts and crafts and a cultural program run for the length of the games.

Snow snake is a game in which an athlete throws a spear as far as possible down a snow channel.

Dogsledding has been a part of life in Nunavut since the arrival of the Thule people from Alaska.

The Kitikmeot Northern Games include many traditional Inuit games, such as the pole twist and various jump kicks.

CANADA

Canada is a vast nation, and each province and territory has its own unique features. This map shows important information about each of Canada's 10 provinces and three territories, including when they joined Confederation, their size, population, and capital city. For more information about Canada, visit **http://canada.gc.ca**.

Alberta
Entered Confederation: 1905
Capital: Edmonton
Area: 661,848 sq km
Population: 3,632,483

British Columbia
Entered Confederation: 1871
Capital: Victoria
Area: 944,735 sq km
Population: 4,419,974

Manitoba
Entered Confederation: 1870
Capital: Winnipeg
Area: 647,797 sq km
Population: 1,213,815

New Brunswick
Entered Confederation: 1867
Capital: Fredericton
Area: 72,908 sq km
Population: 748,319

Newfoundland and Labrador
Entered Confederation: 1949
Capital: St. John's
Area: 405,212 sq km
Population: 508,990

SYMBOLS OF NUNAVUT

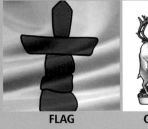

FLAG	COAT OF ARMS	FLOWER
		Purple Saxifrage

0   200   400 Kilometers

0   200   400 Miles

Baffin Bay

Baffin
Island

Davis Strait

Iqaluit
(Frobisher Bay)

Ivujivik

*Labrador
Sea*

NEWFOUNDLAND

Schefferville

Happy Valley-
Goose Bay

Island of
Newfoundland

Chisasibi
(Fort George)

Gander

Saint John's

QUEBEC

Sept-Iles

*Gulf of
St. Lawrence*

St. Pierre and
Miquelon (FRANCE)

Moosonee

Chibougamau

PRINCE
EDWARD
ISLAND

Sydney

Charlottetown

NEW
BRUNSWICK

Fredericton

Quebec

Sudbury

Sherbrooke
Montreal

Saint
John

Halifax

NOVA
SCOTIA

Ottawa

*Lake
Huron*

Toronto
Hamilton
London

*Lake
Ontario*

Lake Erie

Northwest Territories
Entered Confederation: 1870
Capital: Yellowknife
Area: 1,346,106 sq km
Population: 42,940

Nova Scotia
Entered Confederation: 1867
Capital: Halifax
Area: 55,284 sq km
Population: 939,531

Nunavut
Entered Confederation: 1999
Capital: Iqaluit
Area: 2,093,190 sq km
Population: 531,556

Ontario
Entered Confederation: 1867
Capital: Toronto
Area: 1,076,395 sq km
Population: 12,986,857

Prince Edward Island
Entered Confederation: 1873
Capital: Charlottetown
Area: 5,660 sq km
Population: 140,402

Quebec
Entered Confederation: 1867
Capital: Quebec City
Area: 1,542,056 sq km
Population: 7,782,561

Saskatchewan
Entered Confederation: 1905
Capital: Regina
Area: 651,036 sq km
Population: 1,023,810

Yukon
Entered Confederation: 1898
Capital: Whitehorse
Area: 482,443 sq km
Population: 33,442

ANIMAL
Canadian Inuit Dog

TERRITORIAL SYMBOL
Inukshuk

BIRD
Rock Ptarmigan

BRAIN TEASERS

Test your knowledge of Nunavut by trying to answer these boggling brain teasers!

1 Multiple Choice

What is the main industry in Nunavut?
a) agriculture
b) tourism
c) forestry
d) mining

2 Multiple Choice

What percentage of Nunavut's population is Inuit?
a) 5
b) 25
c) 85
d) 99

3 True or False?

All Inuit artwork has an igloo symbol on it to show its authenticity.

4 True or False?

There are many forests and farms in Nunavut.

5 Multiple Choice

In what geographic region is Nunavut found?
a) Canadian Shield
b) cordillera
c) interior plains
d) Hudson Bay lowlands

6 Multiple Choice

How many time zones can be found in Nunavut?
a) 4
b) 2
c) 1
d) 6

7 Multiple Choice

What is the capital of Nunavut?
a) Arviat
b) Iqaluit
c) Igloolik
d) Whale Cove

8 True or False?

Before 1999, Nunavut was part of the Northwest Territories.

1. D, Mining is the main industry in Nunavut. 2. C, The Inuit make up 85 percent of Nunavut's population. 3. False, There are no forests or farms in Nunavut. 4. False 5. A, Nunavut is in the Canadian Shield geographic region. 6. A, Four time zones can be found in Nunavut. 7. B, Iqaluit is the capital of Nunavut. 8. True

MORE INFORMATION

GLOSSARY

bannock: a traditional flatbread

bowheads: a type of whale with a very large head and a lower lip that curves up in a bow on each side

caches: places for storing supplies

Canadian Shield: a region of ancient rock that encircles Hudson Bay and covers a large portion of Canada's mainland

dialects: forms of speech characteristic to certain regions

ecosystem: the relationship between organisms and their environment

eskers: curving ridges of sand or gravel probably deposited by meltwaters

fjords: long, deep, and narrow sea inlets formed by glaciers

game: animals that are hunted for sport

muskeg: an area of swamp or marsh

mutinied: to have rebelled against an authority

narwhals: whales that swim in the Arctic seas; males have a huge tusk that extends from a tooth in the upper jaw.

Northwest Passage: a short-cut route for ships from the Atlantic to the Pacific Ocean

residential: designed for people to live in

serpentine: a green or spotted mineral resembling a serpent's skin

shamans: medicine men or priests believed to have spiritual powers

tridents: spears that have three prongs

BOOKS

Aspen-Baxter, Linda. *Canadian Sites and Symbols: Nunavut.* Calgary: Weigl Educational Publishers Limited, 2004.

Banting, Erinn. *Canadian Aboriginal Art and Culture: Inuit.* Calgary: Weigl Educational Publishers Limited, 2008.

Beckett, Harry. *Canada's Land and People: Nunavut.* Calgary: Weigl Educational Publishers Limited, 2008.

Schwartzenberger, Tina. *Canadian Geographic Regions: The Canadian Shield.* Calgary: Weigl Publishers Educational Limited, 2006.

WEBSITES

Official Nunavut Site
www.nunavut.com

The Nunavut Handbook
www.arctic-travel.com

Government of Nunavut
www.gov.nu.ca

Some websites stay current longer than others. To find more Nunavut websites, use your Internet search engine to look up such topics as "Nunavut," "Iqaluit," "the Arctic," "Inuit," or any other topic you want to research.

INDEX